THE AROMA
OF THAWING

For my son, Rick,
in memory
1985 – 2022

THE AROMA OF THAWING

Poems on Grief and Recovery

SR INCIARDI

I

Unanswerable   11

Soon To Be Lost   12

Uncertainty's Certainty   14

Reflections   15

Cruel Days   16

II

Without Knowing   20

Afternotes   21

Icehouse   22

Purposes   23

The Aroma of Time   24

Contrition   25

The Aroma of Adversity   27

By Dark   28

Hollow Sounds   29

Darkness and Silence   30

Mourning Caves   31

The Aroma of Winter   32

Waiting   33

Sailing   34

Evolvere   35

Dreamers   37

Contentment   38

Voices of the Day   39

Burden's Blessings   40

Faces of Days   42

The Choice   44

III

Forever Wood 46

Winter Endure 48

The Aroma of a New Butterfly 49

Nurture 50

Unlike Another 52

At Night Listening 53

Echoes Through Time 54

Days Like Balloons 55

Remembering Laughter 56

Starlight 57

Sometimes 58

Past Days 59

Can't Say, Can't Know 60

A Made Bed 61

Among Notes at Home 62

Traces 64

IV

Morning Clouds 66

Spring's Aromas 67

And Now 68

Changing Seasons 70

Wind Chimes 71

The Sun's Promise 72

Time March 73

Rain at Night 74

Color 75

Strands 77

Extremes 78

Rain Passing 79

Subtleties 81

Things in Motion 82

Agonous 83

The Aroma of Moonlight's Footsteps 84

Time's Aroma 85

And This 87

Picture Window 88

The Voices of Birds 89

The Aroma of Morning 90

Sunlight at Day's End 91

The Aroma of Thawing 92

About the Author 95

SR Inciardi
The Aroma of Thawing

The Aroma of Thawing is a collection of SR Inciardi's poetry focused on the difficult experience of losing a beloved son, married with two young children, and how a tragic situation (or any situation involving loss, remorse, regret, or betrayal) might be overcome with the help of friends, family, and the natural world.

When we emerge from winter, there is eventually a thawing permitting things to fade away and then remade, enabling robust life to resurface. When the winter finally yields to spring, there is a certain aroma in the air, the thawing water decomposes the leaves and all kinds of organic matter to produce a distinct aroma—evidence of life's resurgence—saying clearly that a change is in the air and, in the end, things will get better even while they can never be the same.

This is his second full collection of poetry.

Enjoy them.

I

Unanswerable

I am angry with you. You were the one
who could have changed it
before it went too far
and when I asked for an answer, was it sacrilege
to expect some sign my pleas were heard,
those made breathlessly in the nights
and through the early mornings,
in the trauma of a time
through my wringing hands and straining voice
calling out to you for help,
oh, please help!
pleading on my knees to protect
a thirty-seven year old's threatened legacies,
in my helplessness crying out
in the deepest darkness under starless skies,
the glowing moon painting the trees
in its palest yellows in stilled air,
my helpless and repeated pleas
throughout those few November nights
without a response,
without the slightest sound.

Soon To Be Lost

Nothing lasts, nothing
can be looked back on
even in light we think stays unchanged
since it too does not remain
as intense as it first was, it does not stay
as robust as when it was first cherished
dressed in its newest colors,
in its textures and fine edges
since nothing sits in the same light
and tells you its story as vibrantly
again and again and again
as when it was first spoken.
In what feels a moment, most of light itself
will lose its sheen.

Time pulses between stilled darkness and lighted motion
and follows this recurring pattern
moving to a place that cannot be retrieved
except in pieces the mind claims,
given up in moments and bursts of memory
fragmented into what no longer sits cohesively,
only they move, carried
by its own tide.

And so I ask: where did my prayers go then,
the ones I made at your bedside
calling for things to return
just as they were, the ones
I shouted in the early mornings
those that came to congeal into a new road,
a road with which I'm unfamiliar,
its parched pavement, its rocky gray contour,
its unevenness my unsure step
along its irregular surface I cannot alter.
And so I ask: where am I headed,
this false hope of returning to where I'd been,
the one I still cling to
even as I see what has passed
in fragments my memory returns
where I see the whole unretrieved
and where the pieces I've lost
are the only ones that hold deeper color.

From what we desire and cannot change
torment comes.

Uncertainty's Certainty

In the absence of warmth
there's little certainty
in the cold stilled breath
of another new morning early
when the sun has yet to climb into sight
but knowing with certainty
it will step above the dark night
and leave no question of its certain light.
But its light for me is forever different
when warmth is absent
and cannot be replenished
while each morning is so much colder,
in bitter cold and silence on a walk alone,
one step after another walking
until I can grasp what I still cannot believe
in the changing angled light of a sun rising,
but how uncertainty thrives in the cold
stilled breath of questions, words, and sounds
still ringing flat by their absence—
cold and certain
as this day's early morning.

Reflections

This is not my life, this cannot be
it, this chaos, this utter dismay
within the body, then out of it,
first across a green meadow
where our walks were immersed
in the swaying grasses of days to come, then alone,
dropped to the tormented sand-thrown shoreline
far below that meadow's edge
sucking the life out of the ocean's calmer waters
abandoned without a way
to scale the rocky walls towering behind me,
in wild nights and ruinous daylight
mourning for the past and the calm meadow waiting—
the calm always given in such modest doses,
then what little given
taken.

Cruel Days

That's it, that's our allotment,
that's what we were given,
a limited bundle of days
wrapped in brown paper,
tied with a coarse cord, what rests inside
a blend of mostly-sunny, unclouded days
some threatening harsh weather,
but taken together, ours alone
wrapped in a package,
and within each of those days,
what we alone were given,
ours alone to have.

There must have been some clock,
some hourglass that ran its course
through the days and nights we believed in
but it's the cruel days that go on
outside our shared allotment,
outside those wrapped in that neat bundle
and set aside from the rest
that burn their mark deep into our souls
telling us bluntly we have little say
in much of anything that matters.

For my son, it was early
in a day in late fall
when not wanting to disturb anyone
in the severe discomfort of a virus
that overtook him, an otherwise healthy person
found weakly breathing
to become the cruelest day
and it was his fate to wait
for the ambulance and arrest not far
from where his two young children were sleeping.

We walk unknowing into the unknown.

Without Knowing

There is no wisdom in what remains mysterious,
when there are so few words to express its absence

and where I anxiously watch the world I'd known
tumble, as if a wingless bird beneath the lost moonlight,

beneath tufted clouds so thick
everything is unable to move.

Where is wisdom when wisdom and its peace
are needed most, when there is nothing

that can be spoken and offered words are stolen
from another moment, when what had thrived

is silenced so abruptly and shadow is the only subtlety?
I cannot speak to what I cannot understand,

know only anger in this time,
its callous mystery, its heartless aftermath,

in the questions that pour out
through the noise of so much silence.

Afternotes

All day I found myself
falling out of daylight
when you would have been thirty-eight,
past the drawn warmth
of the arriving spring's deep sky
and the sun calling,
past the outline
of emerald trees in late day
and the pale rock drawn in sunlight
fading into the dark night,
the other side of what I'd known.
And I am no longer able
to look at daylight in quite the same way
or into what lies ahead and can be
with no sketch drawn and nothing to guide me
only silence without a plan and no sight
just its spreading rim of darkness
suspended by the sound of quiet hesitation
reaching only for questions,
only at the mystery of what had come.

Icehouse

Inside my icy cocoon, my home
crafted of my own design,
the house I've spun
to protect from winter's acrimony,
awaiting the deepening winter-freeze
and speak of the season's indecisions
of comforting dreams in spring's aromas
and so does not reveal itself from within these walls
even as sunlight will melt the snow set upon it.
It's not so much the coming lower temperature
as grief that locks me in place,
the want of moving from what I cannot control
to warmer light teetering between two minds:
what was,
and moving along a path to renewal.
I see only what I know, only know
what is before me unsettled
in this prison that encloses me—
without a whim of what will come.

Purposes

What is it all for these purposes
we assign ourselves to
bringing along and nurturing them
the best we know how to then be
snatched suddenly as if heaven were waiting
with a baited hook
to yank a catch from the water
and just having started upstream
the senseless gathered
and to what end, what purpose?

We are separated by the dense waters of the sea
and I am listening to it in night's darkness
feel its raw breeze hear its unmistakable sighing
what does it say of its purpose or its mortality
where does it go when no one listens
yet I listen
for a calm voice for a grand purpose
in the world of the vulnerable
but this feeling of without is all that comes
the anesthetic of the fog rolling in
its aimless purpose swirling in circles.

The Aroma of Time

In its own moment before I knew
a measure of it carried on slender wings
and what was here or against what had been
and so was aged
fleeing in a smooth slippery coat,
a faceless voice calling out
an echo I heard but once,
once is all I heard it,
its sound moving away
like an anonymous bird in flight
      uncaptured,
           imperfect—
it would not come 'round again.

Contrition

It was one time, just once
when I sat at the water's edge
completely charmed at what I saw:
so much depth and dimension
to what had come to be,
three generations three families
together under an unobstructed sun,
when time was halted so it seemed
and grateful was the only word
I heard myself speaking, when seagulls
swooped along the shoreline
and past, present and all of the future
would be ours.
But that was before Fall
and the change of weather, before I knew
daylight was shrinking
and the rain fell
turning colder, before finite
became a word we'd come to know.
I wish we had more days
at that water's edge, more thoughts
and words spoken aloud.

There always seems to be so much time,
and after a time with any luck,
so much of everything—
> then there isn't.

The Aroma of Adversity

I walk into its dim and hollow halls
hear my hollow footsteps on its cold stone floors,
the hollow walls do not store any wisdom
shared from more tranquil times,
there are no secrets hidden in its mortared stone
but hear unshielded sirens
off in the distance moving closer
shouting anything I might believe.
The earth's trembling hands consume each breath
even as the newest daylight presses against
the morning's window, its voiceless alarm
shouts through it in deafening tones
telling me what I already know,
the clamor of what I know, overtaken
by the noise of so many unanswered questions.

By Dark

Here it comes once more,
drab under an overcast sky
then darkness.
It's the searching
I have not the will to end:
that which was visible,
the absence of what had been
after light dwindles and my attention
is not consumed by other matters.
By dark, I wait in the emptiness,
thinking wherever I am
you'll find me,
speak to me in my pale of sleep
when there is nothing left
to daylight, in the vacant sound
of night waiting
for this void to be filled—
my waiting,
my searching,
my emptiness.

Hollow Sounds

There is only thin air, lifeless air,
the chilled air of seemingly endless days
and a thin mist carrying its hollow sound
in a procession of invisible feet
that overtake my step
moving steadily along its pathway
in late evening and in the early mornings
when light is unformed and without depth
in the emptiness of what I know is missing
and in my anger for its absence.
In the many steps I hear
this hollowness that surrounds each of these days
and presses me to demand
time be rolled back—moments
that will never come again reset
and allowed to be replayed,
the soundlessness and hollow wisdom
somehow filled,
never to be filled.

Darkness and Silence

These are the two fanatics that know my name
thriving beneath what's hidden
holding the power to dwarf the brightest sunlight
and silence the songs and the poet's words
and play unevenly to disquieted ears
when birds stilled by their presence forget
the melodies they were singing
engulfing what only they know,
a place without dimension or wisdom.
I have found them both in these new places
pulled from the sight of bright sky and deep mountain
in the rolling clouds and surging rivers
and in the oceans breaking onto the shores
where I'd belonged
as if the sun had burned its last breath
and merged what remained with my soul.

Mourning Caves

There are no worn paths back
from the caves of mourning
since each path has been overgrown
with dense foliage so tall
the sun is obliterated by them
where any ruts or edges
have been smoothed not by footsteps
but heavy rains so each path out
must be made anew, each path
cut separately from each other
the work hard, the direction unclear
immersed below the tall brush and sharp branches,
below the spiney leaves that tear the skin
where each branch snapped or severed
leaves scars that will remain years after
these isolated caves
in this remote and distant place
I did not care to journey to
awakened as if from a dream
that wasn't a dream at all.

The Aroma of Winter

Thick with anticipation in a time coming
the icy skies filled the canyon with icy water
swirling winds coated the naked trees
in transparent sleeves stripping them of their humor
quaked their frozen souls, the storm's bravado
waged from daylight descending into night
the darkness its evil partner.
At turn of day you are colder than I can believe,
colder than the air of breaths when death has come.
No salvation appears with the newest light,
it is the promise to the soul I want to believe
in hope when hope alone offers no respite
but its aftermath still remains: trees disfigured
by winds, icy winds, downward winds
cracked branches, scattered branches
their dormant limbs shocked writhing and weathered,
limbs of the once firm and vibrant
unable to hear themselves
as if bolts of lightning stiffened by death.

Waiting

The old woman who lives up the road
recently lost her husband,
I found her standing at the edge
of her garden
sobbing,
the pull of the moon held the early morning vapors
she was looking down
looking as if waiting, where the birds sat
on an edge of the rhododendrons she had planted
and the blossoms of the crocuses
had just passed their bloom where each in turn
is arranged at the edge of her tended garden,
its return waiting silently
for the push of April's early rains
held in the still-chilled air of early morning,
and I could see her in this early light
looking down at the edge of her garden
where she stood in the midst of the comings and goings
sobbing.

Sailing

On the night before you sailed from the world
which now holds only yesterday's places,
no one had made any preparation.
It was a chilled fall Monday
before the thanksgiving when thanks
was what everyone we never met was thinking,
little did we know we would not come that far,
we would not raise a glass
as you set out on your journey
across a sea and miles apart
leaving one shore on your way to another
in a deep chilled mist
atop the ocean's swelling belly, hastily
rigging cables and ropes, running lines
and tying knots to secure safe passage
back navigating through the dark narrow channel
past the swoon of mounded grasses
and seagulls circling, heading out
past the edge of the horizon, sailing away,
gone from sight.

Evolvere

And then I came to be
after what had been, the once tall
now withered to the smaller
   after those earlier times.
Many of those times I knew
for the sweetness they brought,
others for the contentment they offered.
   All given, I thought
   lucky to be chosen.
But who was I over all those times?
Where did I go after I had mastered
their gifts:
   in those times given to warmth, the sun
each time unrelenting. I welcomed it,
yet it was the sun itself that imposed its will.
   And in other times given to music,
the newest pieces of what was given
hoarded, unshared
in brilliant sunlight, their melodies too
pressing their will.
When did I come to be
what I am now, a composite refugee,

and will I stay as I am
having come to this, walk in shadows
   unable to hold on,
   unable to grab
and pull you close to my chest?
I hunger for the whys and hows
   of the sounds of your leaving.
And in the years ahead, a search still
and for all those times to come
for what might stay,
   of the thoughts I'd possess,
   those newer ones still unformed,
hoping not to lose myself quietly
to what comes next each time.

Dreamers

All dreamers we are, everyone
scribed to a set of wishes we speak
in the density of the swaying sea's darkness
for what might come to us year after year
as a lamb, shy and meek, comes to nuzzle us
and hand us our destiny.
But destiny shifts in the loose sands
of a reality revealed and ever-changing
while dreamers do what dreamers must,
we are never quite ready
for what comes to replace them.
The pain we cannot foresee for lost dreams
endured like unforgettable eyes
we cannot move past soothed
by the one wish we speak endlessly of—
the one that would have us go back
and replay what played
differently, standing for eternity
in our silence, young as ever.

Contentment

In a dream, contentment was given to me,
in a dream I held it: a small bird
with light and airy feathers, deceptive
in its weightlessness, surprisingly
boney, missing
the mass of any noticeable water.

In a dream, contentment was given to me,
but human as I am, I just couldn't know it,
    I had to own it,
    hold it in my two hands
    as if it could be hoarded,
    be mine alone.
Silently it stayed without a sound,
it did not make any breakable promise,
and like everyone before,
called it bliss, silent peace, sweet living.
But I was wrong
since contentment can move on
as silently as it came, in what seems the silent breath
of one night's moonlight, in the shortest time
to the next daylight, the contentment given in a dream,
    in a dream it had been given,
        had flown on to other places.

Voices of the Day

This is not the first time I've gone back
to the place I'd forgotten, a time
when there was nothing but time
in the narrow Brooklyn streets
and the long summer evenings
and my recollection of stickball between the sewers
in the voices clamoring on the playgrounds of those streets
between the parked cars at each curbside
in those heavy days of sweltering humidity and summer heat
thrashing fire hydrants roaring from their throaty spigots
and how I sought to occupy my time
among the many others I know so little
of what might have happened to them
and of what I could look forward to
rarely on the mind of what I was doing,
in the games played and in the voices of the day while there
what still rests there before time went on unnoticed
and how often I hear her voice calling
out of the blue since you're gone, repeatedly calling
from the top window of our four-story walk-up
back then never hearing her voice calling
me home for dinner.

Burden's Blessings

The loss suggests amputation
a leg now gone, its hollow space, its vulnerability,
even as the nerve endings
twitch, as if the leg that balanced my being
was torn abruptly from its joint.
How am I to go on and carry the weight of this burden?
How am I to see what's missing,
as so many tell me I should,
a blessing—how foolish this concept,
how utterly irrational.
Past the days into months, I see what I had
everywhere: at any dinner table
in a place setting now vacant
or beyond a field of wildflowers
in thick sunlight under the shade
of stretching and dense maple
an abrupt image I might pass by
but where my unconscious memory silently recalls
what was and holds each instance
and I see the blessing in each image,
as painful as they might be, see what I had
and its reminders, since pain is absence

and absence can be soothed when in the mind
nothing had been taken,
however briefly.

Faces of Days

For all the ordinary days that came and went
leaving few marks upon my soul
faded etchings in the chill and the starkness
of a name for days, but not really being days
just a calendar number without a face,
days unremembered for what was and had been,
gathered quietly like bones
in the currents of a river of years,
a boneyard of time piled high,
a jumbled crowd with so few I recognize.
I know they had assembled and wait patiently,
ordinary days sitting not at a beginning or at an end,
unremarkable days seated mostly in the middle
those so alike they fade into the shadows,
one upon another, sketched without color.

What is it about our inability to hold
onto the faces of ordinary days,
in the unknowns and the silence they call out to—
simple ordinary days that pass in anonymity
as if an ancient language I know existed
but am unable to draw upon a single word.

It is a face
but a stranger I cannot recognize.
It is not a face
devoid of any richer facets
that call me to remember.

The Choice

you can mistake it
if you don't listen clearly
it was brief and did not shout
its chance out loud was it better
to have heard it or to have heard it
stop moving toward you
staying briefly then moving away
if you didn't hear it while it was with you
you'll never hear it when it's moved on
and if you never heard it
is it just an echo of the choice
you had but didn't make
that's heard now

III

Forever Wood

It's not that the children were aware
playing in that clubhouse I built when they were younger
when the rear of the house was raw
seeing nothing but brightness in their days
and all that stood and could be seen in that time
and so I went about slicing the lumber
and made the floors and railings mitering the edges
for an extra dose of durability but never thought
in the passing time how it could change and be any different
yet have come to learn thoughts of forever
are just not what thoughts built of wisdom teach
even as cycles of the season's icy winds
or another's soaking rains or a third's blistering heat
conspire to attack the forever-wood to live
in what seems a moment when the sun's brightness
had moved past its peak when the wood's fine grains
and its soaked oils were bleached from it
so what remains is more evident
in the dampness of the dark-green moss thriving
in a less-blinding light I see the wood's once-smooth skin
cracked into deep fissures and see wide fractures
across its now-aged complexion and see its unplanned demise
like any other revealed by the ravages of time

and in the shade from a now-overgrown oak tree's leaves
that stretch over it and through the branches' gentle bow
I know the end of its time has come
even as the leaves hold memory in their youthful hands
and are steadily replaced each year
and so cannot comprehend time's heartlessness
there's no magic in the wood that was
and its new complexion isn't divulged by a name
but can only be seen in the dimming light of what has passed
a long-ago intention cherished for what's now moved on
and for just this shortening time can still be remembered.

Winter Endure

He always said to knock at that fragile door
shadowed in its slender doorway
where howling wind and pelting rains
will slap against its sculpted skin,
peeling the paint from what was sealed
and where once we made our playgrounds
bordered by daffodils in their innocence,
the giddy laughter maturing.

The tumbling seasons have passed
but in our beating hearts
the warmth of the fire of summer endures
caught by the gravity of this winter's cold.
Endure, endure, endure
unlock the door that keeps you captive,
come let me free you from winds
that batter your windowpanes,
come settle into my open arms,
come nestle against my shoulder
so you might weather this season of pain,
your anguish soothed in the brave music
as when I held you as a young child.

The Aroma of a New Butterfly

When I first saw you
you were larger than the towering oak that dwarfed you
that looked into your bluing marble eyes
and didn't know what to make of you—
a large leaf shed from one of its branches?
A huge feather sloughed from the sprawling wing
of an eagle? Certainly not a secret in nature
and any motion in your awkward way,
a slight sigh or thrashing gesture,
bonded to my soul.

In new daylight, our past and present
rolled together when I think back
to your beginning
and in some primitive language
hearing a silent voice say:
"what lives on must relieve
what does not endure"
and how heartless
those silent words sound
yet I realize in all this time,
this is so in everything.

Nurture

when you cried
I came running
abandoning
whatever I had been doing
to put your mind right
and chase the fears from you
I held you
like a bright afternoon
at times I watched
what you could not forget
and helped you
forget
what you had witnessed
holding your age
between my hands
like a quivering bird
offering light
when darkness
is all you saw
and offered
answers

when you hadn't yet
asked questions
on long evenings
with the lights on
into the early morning
and at times
I'm not certain you knew
my presence
when you walked with no need
to reach for my hand
with only a gentle
glance between us
to say in heart-felt words
that make no sound
"Yes, I know"

Unlike Another

How visible you were
to have come only that far
with the light shining through
your hazel-blue eyes and a glow
carried on each of your promises
at once no longer
young and never older with each day
never wasted and to have been
so remembered when your time had gone
as if a gentle wind had stilled the leaves
and they waited for your breath to return
you whom I never confused with any other
and was always surprised at how simply,
quietly, and completely
you could capture anyone's attention
and even the sound of your going
was barely heard, carried
on the calm breeze of so many
silent words listening.

At Night Listening

All the days to come never in my presence
    and the nights hanging
in the air of summer evenings
or the brush of snow tossed by the edge of a board
or the smiles and the bright eyes of children
who cannot speak their loss,
the inertia of each gesture
moves in slower step
    in the ordinary of each day,
in the breaths of a fall afternoon
whose art changes before our eyes
can notice, in the clamor of traffic
moving out of the city,
these are the tickets we'll never again purchase,
the dreams undreamed, the days unlived
together, this is what my heart endures,
in all the days to come
just the thought of you is the closest I will come—
    my flesh, my blood—
to feel your presence in a room,
to know your secret wishes
and grasp fully what it was to love.

Echoes Through Time

You'll know you'll have troubles
when they stop
when you no longer inhale
what the eyes cannot see:
what you'd shared within the same spaces
breathing the same air and what was in it
and that's when you've the most to lose,
that's when if it's stopped
time will stop in any case
and some unseen clock
will have run its course
and your memory will lose
all that was left—
the smiling eyes
the ageless moments you'll still want
to wrap your arms around
those that will bring their colors
for long as you still witness
what is carried on each echo.

Days Like Balloons

All the colorful balloons have gone their separate ways.
Just a portion of them held a cherished moment
tucked inside their delicate skin that rise up to the sky

float and move beyond the sunset, while others burst
to expel their contents and merge
with other days dispersed across a wider field,

their own oxygen slowly gone, their contents
merged into lesser days,
still relieved that this air too had found a home.

From time to time those colorful balloons
that had floated to the sunset, reappear
from the edge of the horizon,

their taut, colorful contours returning
the sights and sounds I once knew
and can vividly recall, their thinly-stretched skins

float in my memory carrying my calm voice
in its preserved skin and bring
memories of days never forgotten.

Remembering Laughter

I now remember laughter
though it's been months
after the grieving late autumn
and long before last daybreak,
in the last time I saw you
us both captured in a photograph,
we two just minding what we enjoyed minding
in the brilliant colors of autumn's afternoon.
Little did I know what would come.
Little did you know why it would end
so abruptly, in the calamity
of autumn's early morning when you still
had countless seasons left, when time unseen
still held its secrets and our words unspoken
held their silence, and the clock stopped
while it was still running,
and all the sun-drenched days to come
are now unwanted. But I alone
will remember laughter, our laughter,
listening for it in the sounds of the old night,
us laughing with our promises, laughing
through our shared disappointment.

Starlight

What the dark sky has known
it has come to share with me,
what it speaks I've come to hear:
hollow sorrow in the sun's absence
without light on earth's contour
or the broadest swaying ocean.
The dark sky hides them equally
where they are masked
from what I had known.
Beyond the sky's darkness, I've learned
to trust the glimmer of stars,
their small hope appearing in their own time
piercing the cover of the dark night void of light
revealing a new way to look at darkness.
I look *for* them and *to* them
to see their bright light and their beauty
redefining absence with their new presence.

Sometimes

Sometimes I dream of the comings and goings
that I can't run past, even as I move
toward consciousness and sometimes
each sit with me in a large soft chair,
perhaps under a light throw, perhaps with a soft melody
playing in the background when both pass
before I can take my next breath.
It is in these times I see their humble purpose
telling me their happiness and their sadness
at the same time, each no different than the other.
Sometimes I dream more about the goings,
about what has walked past the door
as it slowly latched closed, and deeply saddened,
I dream of what could have been,
imagine what had never been
as if it wore the same clothes as its arriving sibling
and I continue to dream where I am seated
along the edge of a narrow stream watching
what comes and seeing what fades
into the gray lip of the horizon—all without sound
without words that convey or express,
and where I thought
one thing would never move on
while I was watching.

Past Days

Would I cherish them if I knew
there would always be more of them
would I cherish them if they were the only ones
I could keep since no more will be made
when many of all days belonged to us
past days recognized from all the others
would I cherish them if what had made them
had not gone so suddenly
if I were blind and hadn't seen them
or deaf and hadn't heard them
and truly knew those past days
in their density and color
would I cherish them if you had been
born someone else or in a different place
or to different people and didn't speak
the private words we shared if they didn't last
even if there were fewer of them
would I cherish any of them if I knew nothing
of the times we were together
nothing at all not even a minute
would I cherish them if we hadn't
cherished them together

Can't Say, Can't Know

I am April in the daylight of the moment,
daylight I've never seen before, but I could be
a day of any month I hold on to. For a time
I travel within them and hold onto some
far longer than their time. I can't say which I will hold on to
and I can't know which I will let go. It remains a mystery
I solve as I go through them.
All month long I've moved toward May.
All month long I've moved toward its more robust light,
its hopeful warmth, its promised progress.
All month long, as with the others, I hold them
young as ever in the palms of my hands, cradle them
like gentle music that blends into the places I've been.
At times, I listen carefully to hear them
as they step from shadows once again.
April holds the ones I hold on to now
mine alone in this time, young as ever.
I know I'll separate some so others
might come forward. I look for new ones
as they come, but never press them.
But I can't say which I will hold on to,
I can't know which I will let go.

A Made Bed

The alternative is still a bed
since what lies on it may be untidy
and arrays its disorder untucked unpulled
at the brighter end of night's waning
it's the fear of fading into obscurity I fear
the amorphous edges the soundless echoes
repeating nothing of what had been
repeating into the silent night
then blending into the early day
day after day as you rose
from a jumbled bed not made
perhaps you were no better off
than when you left it since you left it as it lays,
as it sat when you had last been in it
the legacy if I too should fade away this morning
a misleading sign we were here for however long
but what story would it tell:
the appearance of what we'd left nothing
of what we'd known or what we'd done
but if made—
so much worse.

Among Notes at Home

Hopes and what I had recited from the start
gathered here at home roaming in the arena
of my expectations I see them dancing
in the sounds of a mellow piano in my mind
playing softly in the background
wandering to what is now and from what has passed
and I imagine the fingers scaling the identical keys
yet each sound flowing in new and different sequences
in measures cool water conveys trickling over jagged stones
and what the sounds stir in returning thoughts
of what I had hoped and in what has come to be
I hear them I watch them meander through the rooms
on this Sunday cloaked in the gray-veil of a rainy afternoon.
Were our choices overly blind or not steadfast enough?
Had we scaled the heights of all we could imagine?
To now think back and hear the melodies in my head
note-for-note after the music had stopped
the new sounds now reverberating past hopes
and some melancholy droning to take comfort
in what we had done and in what had come
hearing them play on and how surprised I am
to be carrying these melodies at this time

knowing none of them can be changed
on through each room and from my bed
into the glimmer of morning
where I hear a whisper of them in the notes and keys
of this time as though the oldest music is out of step
with the sounds of what now plays on.

Traces

I remember the sky and clouds
from different days
and in their separate moments
after rolling clouds consumed
the textured blue sky
when I had looked to find
what I know had been there
but could no longer find it
smoothed by the tumbling and its transience
what had been erased by what had been
and it too smoothed by what has come to be
the absence of what had been
floating in air part of the clouds
and a sky that knows nothing of permanence.
But permanence is found in a lasting place
in the images and moments it calls out to
making each of their silent voices heard
carried into all my days remaining
days of longing for which they'll be no ending.

IV

Morning Clouds

Now you seem more daring than I'd noticed.
It is not your bluster but this awe
I can't get past, your effortless movement
guided in secrecy holding my attention
without a sound I watch you playfully float
through this time through this place
seemingly without an end to your distance
and I recall the many times
I've longed to look up and capture your soul
but from far below can only watch
as you skate and take shape quietly
leaving me to think:
you must hold the secret of youth
following paths only you can follow
and how each moment brings renewal
while I know I cannot reset the limits
of my being here in what I've known
or in what you can't help me change.

Spring's Aromas

The softening appears everywhere
and at once I want to join it,
kneel down and place my palms
upon the earth's cool skin,
feel its breathing, its awakening
when the grasses are greening
and the shrubs and tall trees
push the early leaves to the tips of their fingers.
But among all this, surges
of grief still come, where the deep freeze
of winter's isolation still clutches
sadness and pierces hopefulness.
My eyes see this new place
and I can smell the spring's aromas
carried on the warmer air
and they both, at least in those moments,
take me from what I cannot get over,
what I know I will never get over.

And Now

And now it has at once ended
what I thought I'd forever be held by
and what would never be relinquished,
what in my head had led me to believe
the deep and shadowed forests
would remain hushed and stay unknown
on grainy contoured beaches that would
stay cleansed by the surf's white-water will
what I had seen and had heard
but know and hear it now more clearly
among the birds clamoring in the certain sunlight
among deer who return with their quizzical stares
to then graze along the edges of a sloping hill
its story has come and it has resumed silently.
I had believed I'd find it
had heard and understood
it could be found in the weighty sounds
the snow-peaked mountains made
in the riotous streams running down
tearful cheeks and in whose voices
raised their thrashing arms to call out
wherever they were
in all of those days now ended

and pass their will in the silence of a new morning
and recognize through this solemn time
the few sounds I can decipher
like music from quieted pianos now playing
in silent songs I still cannot name
but in new melodies I've now come to know.

Changing Seasons

Just past midway between the two solstices
I smell it
in the scent of the air's changing aroma,
when the air still carries its winter chill
yet when signs of a new spring season emerge,
in the greener grasses and in the expanding light
that lengthens what had been cut short.
I hear it
in the birds singing in the early morning's darkness
before light spreads across the horizon
when it will lift them to greater intensity,
even while the chill still captures and holds
all that it surrounds, through the many moments
of my sadness when what has been lost
still consumes what is carried into the day.
I hear it
beyond what I can see,
out in the still-lifeless trees
singing songs they want to share
well before the buds come and then the flowers
and just as the ground is softening.
I smell it.
    I hear it.
        I know it.

Wind Chimes

I believe it is dissent pushing from the sky
what is warmer and in what is colder under clouds,
the warmth rising, the chilled shadow falling
transformed to wind
stirring across the valley onto the plains
and across the meadow
to rustle the dense trees at its edge
and set a force in motion:
encouraging what continues,
or in overwhelming strength,
what does not. These are my days
formed by the will of the wind,
by its choices I will never grasp
but can only witness
in the movement of branches
and in the quiver of leaves,
the air moving to the place it will go to
despite where it may be unwelcome
my porch-hung wind chimes
hanging from the rafters
an echo of proof telling when it's come,
and in silence the sound of when it's gone.

The Sun's Promise

after sunset when darkness comes
it's the sun that makes its promise
spoken in a hushed lullaby a quiet pledge
to hold its light steady
at what it knows is just our speed
but not heed our hopes to move any faster
despite our pacing for time to pass
for whatever our reasons or in other moments
our wishing to turn around
and go back and replay what had been
for it's the sun that never changes
remaining where it left us
and knows both our vagaries and our limitations
as an attentive parent would describe our reason
and not pretend other days had not passed
or think time could somehow be cleared
to begin again—the sun knows better
than to begin again since it knows time speaks
its newest words once in just one direction
and never a circle even as the names
for the days and months begin
fresh in every cycle

Time March

You are gone from where we were
younger, then older
in the sights and notions
we shared, it was
the shortest time
in a time not counted
in images I'll hold on to
the absence of new ones noticed
like birds gone in winter
until just moments are recalled
in the pubs and places
and every manner of days
we were together.
This is the risk in loving
another, as vulnerable
defines the word 'alive',
as it defines existence.
I know what I'm missing.
I know I'm the one
who carries the moments
in their colors, but as much
as it will have to do
it will not be enough
yet against the alternative,
the only choice worth taking.

Rain at Night

Its will has come to take what I'd known
in broad sunlight when all I could see
was sunlight and what stood in it,
cleansing the vividness
once the night's rainwater had come.
And I recall what was, the sunlight
bringing color and density
to what my eyes made clearer,
and I recall the sun painting
the day's common gray walls
in diverse colors and the bland
still-browned grasses awakening
and growing richer, where now I wait
late into the night for the end
of the steady rain to pass
   without contrition, without amends
waiting to see the day's sunlight return
bringing its new color to the morning
and what it will then will to leave behind.

Color

It is the variety that is surprise,
yet still in a range of similar colors: deep blue
yielding to a different shade of blue,
the hint of dark green and muted purple,
not of the range of rainbow
but a more subtle variety
those closer to each other
yet distinguishable from each to each.
Why now? What's changed—just the solace
of the familiar returning,
I see its variety in my mood
awakening to this new range of color
where there had been but one,
past the sadness of the music floating in air
shifting to a stronger energy.
I do not believe the music alone
teaches, but notice its movement
just as I see the colors move. In my own time
I accept my vulnerability:
having had so much to lose
captured by the breathlessness
of its absence, yet aware

this is true of everything—
what we have is ours but a moment
so that what we knew can return to us
in surprise.

Strands

It's the small urgings I feel now,
the strands of a usual world
spinning beyond the dark night
and into the new morning, the urge to start
what had been too heavy to push,
this new unseating, this lift from the edge
to walk outside and restart what had been abandoned.
It's the small nudges that talk to me now
in brief sentences, I hear them in simple words
not to build a colossal bridge from here to what had been,
but in smaller strands with words more lasting
carrying what I will come to place on them,
stick by stick, strand by strand, each lesser-weighted
than the denser brick that's been put aside.
Its callousness, its turmoil
softened by a new usual, in new patterns
and humble steps, walking myself
into my best sentences, speaking my own words,
my own thoughts sketching a picture
of this new place coming,
a place from which I can be remade.

Extremes

Vacant nests sit in the crooks of high branches
but birds are singing everywhere,
their pitched voices sing to a new season
on the step of just one day,
one turn of the earth and it's as if the day
arrived to open into a new world.
And I am here in this new place
in what seems like a moment
taking it in, taking it into the palms of my hands
while I know the world I moved from
the old world I left will never leave me.

From what we do not limit extremes are made.

Rain Passing

The rain has stopped falling through the trees
sitting at this lonely window hearing
what an old man said he'd seen come and go
hearing what he'd uttered in a silent voice
the words he himself had spoken
carried from an age to a new age
I spoke some of those words with him
in new breaths the old way no longer recognized
the grainy phrases we barely share now spoken.
See how far away and how long ago the raindrops fell,
they no longer coat the trees
in the same ways he once saw,
they are no longer held
by the tips of the leaves in the same way
once the rain had passed
when there is nothing else to hear
when the soundless night echoes through the dark trees
and the linguists speak their newer words
and close the pages on the old ones
only an old man can remember.

The rainclouds have dropped their moisture
and the ground beneath the leaves is soaked
by it and where from it the newest words will sprout
and speak into my newest living ears.

Subtleties

It's what I discern long after I've looked
hidden in the blankets of what comfort me,
its warmth, its caress
when callousness still surrounds most everything
my eyes might gaze upon,
it is in the subtleties of early morning
when light seeps along the edges of the window shades,
when what was a maze of brown and beige
offers hints of spring's thin coat of green.
These are the subtleties I discern,
these are sights I'm drawn to,
not to have forgotten what had been
but cherish what still lives on.

I cannot change what cannot be changed,
I cannot move what cannot be moved:
the ocean's powerful roar, its crashing waves,
its dense curling water,
the blue colors shading the distant mountains,
and the eagles flying, the air swirling
putting sound to their swooping wings.
The air I breathe.
The air I know.

Things in Motion

After thoughts have subsided and the artist's brush
is dabbed into the palette's deeper colors
and it begins to stroke the canvas' textured skin,
you can hear the motion gone from any voice heard
but art goes on dancing in the eyes of a child
since to a child all things are in motion,
all things rumble across the earth
like the wall-art of ancient caves,
in the deer running and the horses moving
in their smooth exchanges taken as they are
and for what they say in intensity
not in the modern splatter of certain days
but in colorful blots painted abruptly
in the moments we live for,
those sketches not moving,
those that remain frozen, stuck in time
for eternity.

Agonous

Assurance comes after hopefulness.
Who can argue that we were destined
to be challenged even as we were born
into it and still not know what comes
and who cannot say they know
its somber color, its heavy shadow
lifted by our two shoulders
carrying the weight of what must be,
consoled by everyone that an end will come.
Yet we carry it for who knows how long
and for that time is the only time
changed only by the definition of its edges,
the dark colors holding it in the field
of a painter's faded blottesque style, and survives
despite our wishes. Its deep hues, its dark variations
speak to what it alone knows and at times
continues beyond our fair share.
Yet we must bear down
and long for what sits beyond those days
and for what remains unseen, hungering
for the end, we seek to change it
or we alone surrender.

The Aroma of Moonlight's Footsteps

That is the way it now moves,
not in motions distinct from each other
where in a moment one carries nighttime's weight alone
until the next one can be placed down,
but more as a lamp would come to glow
across earth's seamless floor
through a sheer gown where light from behind
might illuminate what's ahead
and where lesser light remains unaware
of other times or other ages.
Its moonlight will not clang like a school steeple's bell
but will speak its mind in whispers and hushed voices
spoken under an ancient amber glow,
what the eyes have come to know,
where its voice speaks of many pasts
and the sounds they made:
the many fragments blending to be everything
and how this comes to be the only thing
worth longing for.
And for all that is known and for what it now calls out to
in the vast darkness of the night's silent sky
an apparition, an ageless voice
muffled by a folded hand, muffled of its silent will
so just its newest whispers might be heard.

Time's Aroma

We've long thought there would always be time
and that time ahead
was stored in abundance, sometimes wasted,
sometimes used in regrettable moments,
but we could not imagine running out of it,
the thought of going back through it
rarely on our minds. We usually found ourselves
looking out to time to come,
since we spent little time
dwelling on what had happened.

But now the time ahead is an empty space
since your laughter and your smile have gone,
I guess our allotment was met
and we no longer have it to share
among the orange sunsets of what was,
in the green pastures we walked together,
in the wet sand where we talked
near the ocean's swell casting its moist breath
in our faces,
we have been here and it has shifted.

So this is time's aroma. This is the essence
of what sits silently, yet I'm made more aware of it,
and see how it is there
in just one moment at a time through time,
not early or late to appear
that there is only one of it running in a straight line,
its aroma in the air I alone now fly through,
in the changing trees and in the changing skies,
in the waters of its constant motion,
in the noise confusion might surround any minute,
and how its aroma too remembers and whispers
of what has passed and of what goes on
as it moves forward while moving backward
for us from our time, all the time I will most cherish
for as long as my time still moving
on alone permits.

And This

See how the redbreast assembles her nest
even in the oddest places
here beneath the cover of hanging impatiens
camouflaged from the sun's revealing eyes
yet unshielded from the threat of rushing rain
with three blue eggs touching their lips
a miniature star I might miss entirely
until an opening between the stalks reveals them
when she then alarms the world I've approached
from a safe branch of hemlock just far enough away
and goes about what appears she's been taught
without words or another example
in no other place but this place
knowing well what goes on
within the edges of this warm ordinary day
wrapped by night yielding to morning
and the day folding back to night
and the whole just the whole
as simple and as complex as it needs to be.

Picture Window

It looks out to what it sees
a passing early-spring rain ending,
tears streaking its glossy cheeks
watching deer redbreasts squirrels
move in their soggy rituals
and fill its frame like a diorama in motion
the background tinted
by the weakened grip of winter,
the color of bland sitting in silence
speaking in the more common words
of nature's full intention.
I see the slightest movements now,
understand my mother's lessons
on how everything that endures speaks silently,
how color is at its best when muted
most comforting when framed
in the texture of rituals.

The Voices of Birds

I hear them drawn to their commitments
those birds on the bobbing branches
singing their constant early-morning melodies
seemingly inside that one tree
tucked in the corner of my yard,
how in the budding daylight, they seem to dwell
on just beginnings day-after-day
in voices playful as ever. I listen to their tireless song
when in the coming years
all I'll know is the quiet of my own lost voice.
So what should I care
about the voices of birds, those melodies have played
and will still be playing, still be heard
on many future mornings. What do I know
of what is finished or of what continues?
All I know is their voices go on
unaware anyone hears them,
and how I keep returning to this ambiguity,
their voices singing determinedly to unknown ears
in the same melodies and in the same tones
the whole time committed to survive and carry forward
what they've learned to have worked for centuries.

I will listen to their music into another life.

The Aroma of Morning

It arrives a shy handmaiden
stepping softly across the meadow
whispering under a breath of sunlight
touching it lifting it with gentle influence
with widening eyes reaching to promise
an inquisitive child quelling fear
grasping confidence. I watch her transform
a gentle flower sprouting to proudly reveal
her bold color moving across the foothills
stepping lightly into the meadow
a grand transition in the sweet aroma
of a vibrant princess her confidence,
      her demeanor,
majestic.

Sunlight at Day's End

I will see it for as long as I am here,
a cherished sight nudging a subtle breeze
softly touching what it reaches to touch
the dimming angled light of another day passing
and I am here captured in this dimming light
by what passes in each day
and how it is returned exactly how it left
exactly how I saw it when I left it
exactly how it is again in the new morning
but not all things return as they were
in time what's seen forms different shapes
over seasons' changes and over longer times
a mighty oak that may have silently fallen
is returned as a small cluster of softer Bradford Pear
their thinner delicate leaves their more subtle branches
similar yet distinct from what had been
I know what was and what is now
I see what has come and what has gone
both trees having been cast
in the subtle sunlight at day's end
but can remember in subtle hues
the dense oak just the same.

The Aroma of Thawing

Remember when the milder winds
floated through the leafless trees
and the sounds they made were less hollow?
Remember how what needed thawing
at once knew both loss and its unfairness,
and just because it was listless inside
didn't mean it would stay permanently so
since what can be thawed will,
won't forever stay quelled.
In time and under more receptive conditions,
what was frozen will emerge
when least expected
in a burst of milder weather
even if the returning chill of a moonless night
may cause its refreezing
at once dormant yet breathing softly
so that what can be thawed
will thaw in its own time.

Cast from the things I'd known
to the things I've come to see,
an open window or a short walk
can infuse wisdom beyond words

when encircled
by the released aroma of thawing
freed from the earth to move on
so we might inhale it with each new breath,
freeing us too for the moment
from what holds us in its grip.

About the Author

SR (Salvatore Richard) Inciardi was born in New York City and attended Brooklyn College and New York University. He worked in health care in New York and in New Jersey for close to 40 years. All the while SR Inciardi has been writing poetry and attempting to perfect his writing interests. He has been heavily influenced by Robert Frost and WS Merwin among other poets like Billy Collins and Louise Gluck. SR Inciardi has been married since 1978 and has one married adult child and four grandchildren.

This is SR Inciardi's second collection of poetry. The first, *Coloring Outside the Edges*, was released in October 2022 and has been made available on Amazon, Apple Books, Walmart, Barnes & Noble and other outlets including an eBook version released at the same time.

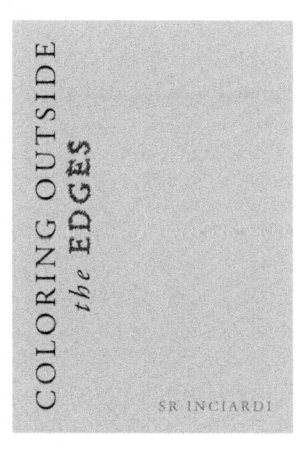

Copyright © 2023 SR Inciardi

All rights reserved. No part of this book may be reproduced or used in any manner without the prior written permission of the copyright owner, except for the use of brief quotations in a book review.

ISBN: 979-8-9881543-0-3
Paperback ISBN: 979-8-9881543-4-1
eBook ISBN: 979-8-9881543-1-0

First Edition 2023

Cover & Interior Design by Liliana Guia
Cover Photo 119596006 © Olga Dmitrieva | Dreamstime.com

Printed in Great Britain
by Amazon